OBOE
PATRIOTIC FAVORITES

Solos and Band Arrangements
Correlated with Essential Elements Band Method

Arranged by
MICHAEL SWEENEY

Welcome to Essential Elements Patriotic Favorites! The arrangements in this versatile book can be used either in a full concert band setting or as solos for individual instruments. The SOLO pages appear at the beginning of the book, followed by the BAND ARRANGEMENT pages. The supplemental CD recording or PIANO ACCOMPANIMENT book may be used as an accompaniment for solo performance.

ISBN 978-0-634-05013-8

HAL•LEONARD®
CORPORATION
7777 W. BLUEMOUND RD. P.O. BOX 13819 MILWAUKEE, WI 53213

00860084

AMERICA, THE BEAUTIFUL

OBOE
Solo

Words by KATHERINE LEE BATES
Music by SAMUEL A. WARD
Arranged by MICHAEL SWEENEY

BATTLE HYMN OF THE REPUBLIC

Words by JULIA WARD HOWE
Music by WILLIAM STEFFE
Arranged by MICHAEL SWEENEY

OBOE
Solo

00860084

GOD BLESS AMERICA®

OBOE
Solo

Words and Music by
IRVING BERLIN
Arranged by MICHAEL SWEENEY

MY COUNTRY, 'TIS OF THEE
(America)

Words by SAMUEL FRANCIS SMITH
Music from THESAURUS MUSICUS
Arranged by MICHAEL SWEENEY

OBOE
Solo

THIS IS MY COUNTRY

Words by DON RAYE
Music by AL JACOBS
Arranged by MICHAEL SWEENEY

OBOE
Solo

HYMN TO THE FALLEN

Music by JOHN WILLIAMS
Arranged by MICHAEL SWEENEY

OBOE
Solo

YANKEE DOODLE/YANKEE DOODLE BOY

OBOE
Solo

Traditional
Arranged by MICHAEL SWEENEY

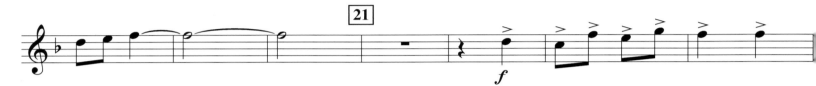

From the Motion Picture THE PATRIOT
THE PATRIOT

Composed by JOHN WILLIAMS
Arranged by MICHAEL SWEENEY

OBOE
Solo

00860084

ARMED FORCES SALUTE

OBOE
Solo

Arranged by MICHAEL SWEENEY

STARS AND STRIPES FOREVER

By JOHN PHILIP SOUSA
Arranged by MICHAEL SWEENEY

OBOE
Solo

THE STAR SPANGLED BANNER

OBOE
Solo

Words by FRANCIS SCOTT KEY
Music by JOHN STAFFORD SMITH
Arranged by MICHAEL SWEENEY

AMERICA, THE BEAUTIFUL

OBOE
Band Arrangement

Words by KATHERINE LEE BATES
Music by SAMUEL A. WARD
Arranged by MICHAEL SWEENEY

00860084

BATTLE HYMN OF THE REPUBLIC

OBOE
Band Arrangement

Words by JULIA WARD HOWE
Music by WILLIAM STEFFE
Arranged by MICHAEL SWEENEY

GOD BLESS AMERICA®

OBOE
Band Arrangement

Words and Music by
IRVING BERLIN
Arranged by MICHAEL SWEENEY

00860084

MY COUNTRY, 'TIS OF THEE
(America)

OBOE
Band Arrangement

Words by SAMUEL FRANCIS SMITH
Music from THESAURUS MUSICUS
Arranged by MICHAEL SWEENEY

THIS IS MY COUNTRY

OBOE
Band Arrangement

Words by DON RAYE
Music by AL JACOBS
Arranged by MICHAEL SWEENEY

00860084

From the Paramount and DreamWorks Motion Picture SAVING PRIVATE RYAN

HYMN TO THE FALLEN

OBOE
Band Arrangement

Music by JOHN WILLIAMS
Arranged by MICHAEL SWEENEY

YANKEE DOODLE/YANKEE DOODLE BOY

OBOE
Band Arrangement

Traditional
Arranged by MICHAEL SWEENEY

From the Motion Picture THE PATRIOT

THE PATRIOT

Composed by JOHN WILLIAMS
Arranged by MICHAEL SWEENEY

OBOE
Band Arrangement

ARMED FORCES SALUTE

Arranged by MICHAEL SWEENEY

OBOE
Band Arrangement

00860084

STARS AND STRIPES FOREVER

By JOHN PHILIP SOUSA
Arranged by MICHAEL SWEENEY

OBOE
Band Arrangement

THE STAR SPANGLED BANNER

OBOE
Band Arrangement

Words by FRANCIS SCOTT KEY
Music by JOHN STAFFORD SMITH
Arranged by MICHAEL SWEENEY

00860084

MORE FAVORITES FROM ESSENTIAL ELEMENTS

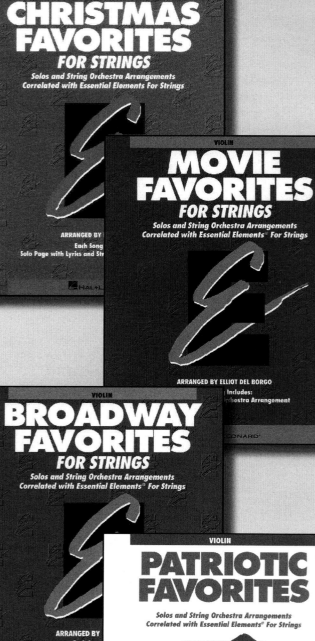

These superb collections feature favorite songs that students can play as they progress through their string method books. Each song is arranged to be played by either an orchestra or by soloists, with optional accompaniment on CD.

Each song appears twice in the book, featuring:
• Solo instrument version
• String arrangement for orchestra or ensembles
• Accompaniment CD included with conductor's score
• Accompaniment CD available separately
• Piano accompaniment book that is compatible with recorded backgrounds

Available:
• Conductor
• Violin
• Viola
• Cello
• String Bass

• Accompaniment CDs
• Value Starter Pak
  (includes 24 Student books
  plus Conductor Book w/CD

CHRISTMAS FAVORITES
Arranged by Lloyd Conley
Songs include:
The Christmas Song
  (Chestnuts Roasting
  on an Open Fire)
Frosty the Snow Man
A Holly Jolly Christmas
Jingle-Bell Rock
Let It Snow! Let It Snow! Let It Snow!
Rockin' Around the Christmas Tree
We Wish You a Merry Christmas

BROADWAY FAVORITES
Arranged by Lloyd Conley
Songs include:
Beauty and the Beast
Cabaret
Edelweiss
Get Me to the Church on Time
I Dreamed a Dream
Go Go Go Joseph
Memory
The Phantom of the Opera
Seventy Six Trombones

MOVIE FAVORITES
Arranged by Elliot Del Borgo
Includes themes from:
An American Tail
Chariots of Fire
Apollo 13
E.T.
Forrest Gump
Dances with Wolves
Jurassic Park
The Man from Snowy River
Star Trek
Mission: Impossible

PATRIOTIC FAVORITES
Arranged by John Moss
Songs include:
America, the Beautiful
Battle Hymn of the Republic
God Bless America
Hymn to the Fallen
My Country, 'Tis of Thee (America)
The Patriot
The Star Spangled Banner
Stars and Stripes Forever
This Is My Country
Yankee Doodle

FOR MORE INFORMATION, SEE YOUR LOCAL MUSIC DEALER,
OR WRITE TO:

HAL•LEONARD®
CORPORATION
7777 W. BLUEMOUND RD. P.O. BOX 13819 MILWAUKEE, WI 53213
Visit Hal Leonard Online at **www.halleonard.com**

Prices, contents, and availability subject to change without notice.
Some products may not be available outside the U.S.A.

0210